D1231188

Published and Distrubted by Life Science Publishing
www.DiscoverLSP.com
1218 South 1850 West, STE A
Orem, Utah 84020

# ACKNOWLEDGMENTS

*First I would like to give my husband a huge THANK YOU! He takes my thoughts and puts them into words that make sense to others. He is a brilliant editor.*

*Next, my daughter Emily who drew the concept art for the cover and to the Graphic Artist who made it into reality!*

*I appreciate Dr. Dan Purser, Gary Young and Marc Schroeder for the Progessence Plus formula that is changing lives all over the world! These men are brilliant!*

*Thanks to all my clients who experimented with Progessence Plus and gave me feedback so we could write the Troubleshooting page!*

*I am indeed extremely grateful for my children and my friends who put up with me when I am in production mode! They are patient and kind and supportive. I couldn't do this without them.*

*Thank you Lynne Klippel from "Love Your Life Publishing" for teaching me how to write books!*

*I am grateful to God for His Inspiration and Guiding Influence in my life and business.*

*And especially, a great big THANK YOU THANK YOU THANK YOU to Jason Dang from Life Science Publishing for getting this book published!*

# TESTIMONIALS

*"Hi, I'm from México. I admire your work and I love essential oils too."*
Carmen Garibi

*"I just read the most fascinating e-book, Taming the Dragon Within, by Drs. LeAnne & David Deardeuff, DC. This book is a must read for women of all ages, early teen through post menopausal.*

*The doctors give natural solutions for hormonal imbalances, Chronic Fatigue syndrome, allergies, thyroid, infertility, miscarriages, anxiety & depression, musculo-skeletal problems and a myriad of other ailments with the recommendations of YLEO essential oils & supplements.*

*In Dr. LeAnne's many years of working with women she found that many have gone through years of pain and frustrations and not to mention thousands of dollars spent to get better only to feel the same or grow worse. Some have been misdiagnosed or simply overlooked.*

*If you are ready to embark on the journey to your best healthy life, let Drs. LeAnne and David show you how."*
Judi Gephart

*"Dr. LeAnne you are brilliant! I am so happy! You really changed my body by bringing me back to hormone balance! I will continue to stay on the protocol you gave me! Your books are incredible.*
*I love all of them!!!!"*
Maria Billis

*"Just bought it (Taming the Dragon Within)! And today I received your book "Ultimate Balance" in the mail. I guess I had better finish reading "Inner Transformations Using Essential Oils" first. It is great, by the way."*
Sharon Escott Brigance


*"Thanks for all you do for us. I do appreciate you."*
Melody Moon

*"When I have a health concern, I typically ask upline, because they have been generous in their time in educating me for so many years. The only exception to this is when I pay for a personal consultation with Dr. LeAnne Deardeuff, DC. She has solved in a few months a skin issue that the medical doctors could not solve in several years. She has given my mother the tools to turn around a scary diagnosis such that by the time of the next testing, the docs could find no evidence of the original diagnosis.*

*Out of all the people I know to turn to for advice when I don't know what to do or when what I'm doing isn't working, I turn to Dr. LeAnne because her recommendations have given me and my family success so many times in the past. I'd like to recommend her two books:*

· *Inner Transformations Using Essential Oils: Powerful Cleansing Protocols for Increased Energy and Better Health*
· *Ultimate Balance: Infusing the Vibrational Energy of Essential Oils into Chakras, Meridians and Organs*

*Hopefully, you will never have a need to contact her, but if you have a challenging health issue, she is an extremely valuable resource."*
Kathryn Caywood

# INTRODUCTION

Dragons are notorious for being angry, menacing, fire-breathing forces of destruction. I know all about dragons through films and fantasy books, and sometimes I feel like one lives inside me!

Dragons are hot. By this I don't mean that they are good-looking; rather that they are a constant burning furnace. Also, dragons tend to sleep a lot and have voracious appetites, sometimes eating as much as an entire cow every day! Dragons are known to be extremely moody and prone to bursts of temper that involve bursts of flame and lashing out with their tail! It is never wise to anger a dragon!

Smaug, from Tolkien's *The Hobbit*, hoarded vast amounts of treasure deep within a cave. He was extremely jealous and protective of this treasure and wouldn't share with a single soul. One day Smaug discovered a thief had stolen something from him and in retribution destroyed an entire village! (Some people say that if a woman were ever president there would be war every 28 days! No matter how little the provocation there would be war. Period.) Dragons are HUGE! They must drink an incredible amount of water to cool themselves down, so their bellies are always distended. Look at Elliot, AKA Pete's dragon! Elliot was tremendously rotund. Elliot was also very shy and reserved (a dragon characteristic not always recognized). Elliot had a mischievous sense of humor and loved to tease people.

There are also the magic dragons like Puff (from the famous song) and Ancaladar (my favorite dragon from the *Obsidian Trilogy* by Mercedes Lackey). Puff loved to frolic, while Ancaladar was benevolent. Ancaladar hid in a cave for years so as not to be discovered and killed. While there he became friends with, and bonded with, an elf. Because of this dragon's love for the elf and others Ancaladar bestowed the elf with gifts of magic to benefit and serve mankind. Ancaladar had made an oath to protect mankind, much as Draco from *DragonHeart* had. Draco took the oath so seriously he gave his life to save people from tyranny.

In the recent film H*ow to Train your Dragon,* a boy found a wounded dragon and did all he could to heal and love it. He found the dragon's ticklish spots and areas it loved to have rubbed; he healed its wounds and helped it learn how to fly again; and he found, most importantly, that the dragon LOVED fish. The boy learned that any kind of dragon could be tamed by first taking care of its needs and being kind and loving.

So how are women like dragons? So much is obvious! We are living furnaces; we are moody, blowing up at the littlest things one day and being calm and controlled the next; we are full of love and service and are tremendously loyal to those we love; some days of the month we are starving hungry; some days we have headaches and cramps; some days we take in so much water we puff with edema and water weight; sometimes we seem to explode around the middle like Elliot; and sometimes we are exhausted and need to sleep a lot.

So how do we tame this inner dragon? This book is on how to balance our hormones so that our fiery dragon is put to sleep and the other side, the kind side, can emerge and take over.

# Taming the Dragon Within

### Hormones are the fire that makes the dragon.

They are produced by the endocrine system, are a vital part of our physical bodies. As you will see as you read this booklet, understanding the role hormones play and learning to keep them in balance is vital to taming the dragon within. (growl)

The beautifully complex endocrine system of the body includes many glands that are familiar to most people as well as some that are less well known. In this booklet we are going to focus on issues surrounding the primary women's sex hormones, which are made in the ovaries, the adrenals, the placenta and even the lining of the gut.

What all endocrine glands have in common is the production of hormones to direct the metabolic functions of the body. Although each gland produces its own particular hormone(s), they all affect each other either directly or through feedback mechanisms. For the most part this all takes place via secretions of surprisingly tiny amounts of hormones that are carried to the target tissue via the bloodstream.

It must also be noted that in addition to feedback mechanisms, the liver also is heavily involved in the endocrine system as it constantly removes excess hormones of all types from the blood stream. This complex interrelationship of the endocrine glands and indeed all the systems of the body often makes diagnosis of a person's condition difficult. For example, chronic fatigue or a nervous breakdown can stem from a hormone imbalance. (snore)

Before we can intelligently discuss the sex hormones themselves, we must address the glands "upstream" from the sex glands that produce hormones that have a controlling effect on them. We will start at the top (literally and functionally) with the hypothalamus.

### The hypothalamus
Dragons can be extremely moody. It starts here.

The hypothalamus is the primary regulatory center of the body. It is an area deep in the center of the brain that receives chemical signals through the blood and electrical signals through the nervous system that together keep it up to date on the body's condition and needs. It is involved in regulating just about all moment-to-moment, day-to-day metabolic functions of the body.

The hypothalamus not only keeps track of blood concentrations of hormones, water, electrolytes and nutrients, but also receives an "info" copy of practically every nerve impulse that is transmitted in the body, even including emotion-laden thoughts. Thus it may be seen that the hypothalamus, located right in the middle of the limbic system, is where our emotions interface with the nervous and endocrine systems to affect bodily functions and health.

Thanks to this interplay of emotional, nerve and endocrine signals, it often happens that a person in a state of intense feeling will cause whatever the particular emotion may be to be sent to its corresponding organ, to interfere with its function and to be stored there. This is not conventional, modern Western thinking, but the linking of emotions with organs can be traced back to at least Biblical times.

It is unfortunate that the emotions that affect us most strongly are usually negative. **(roar)** The effect of these negative emotions on the associated organs can cause diseases of various kinds that cannot be cured until the emotional component is dealt with. Some of the emotions traditionally associated with particular organs are:

- Fear, worry .......................................... kidney
- Anger, rage ........................ liver, gall bladder
- Inner crying .......................... lungs or kidney
- Sadness ............................................ pancreas
- Lack of joy ............................................ heart
- Unforgiveness ......................................... liver
- Revenge ............................... kidney (stones)
- Stress ............................................... stomach
  (also may affect the immune system)

Beyond the effect on specific organs, positive as well as negative emotions influence the whole organism – body, mind and soul.

Interestingly, the hypothalamus has a direct connection from the olfactory organs of the nose **(snort)**, i.e., our sense of smell. This occurs by way of cranial nerve I, which, alone among the cranial nerves, is actually an extension of the brain tissue. This situation, found nowhere else in the nervous system, means that the things we smell pass directly into the brain without any intermediate synapses.

But in order for any scent to be recognized by the brain, it must be carried in a lipid – an <u>oil</u>. What a unique and powerful opportunity this provides to use essential oils to impact the brain and body quickly. Studies have shown that this does indeed occur; scents held below the nose show up instantly in the hypothalamus. Thus we see the very real opportunity for treatment of all sorts of ills through the use of aromatherapy.

Now let's discuss the three glands that direct energy usage in the body: the pituitary, the thyroid and the adrenals.

**The pituitary gland**
Dragons try to get as much sleep as they can.

A damaged pituitary gland can cause the need to sleep a lot – and a lot of other problems as well.

The pituitary gland has often been called the master gland of the body although, given what we know about the hypothalamus, it should probably be called the executive officer. It gets its orders from the hypothalamus through hormonal as well as nerve signals, and then sends its own hormonal secretions to the other endocrine glands, directing them to produce their respective hormones or to send out signals to yet other glands.

The pituitary also produces several hormones that have a direct effect on the body, including human growth hormone (HGH).

The pituitary secretes hormones that stimulate the ovaries or testes to produce their respective hormones, the kidneys to control water retention, and the adrenal glands to produce various adrenocorticotropins. In women, the pituitary also signals the uterus to promote contraction at the time of childbirth and the mammary glands to produce milk after childbirth, and it is heavily involved in regulating the monthly cycle.

Given the pituitary's pre-eminence in controlling the other glands of the body, it is obvious that hypopituitarism (an under-performing pituitary gland) will have tremendous effects on the overall health of the individual. If the executive officer of the endocrine system is not functioning properly, the other glands and organs will not function properly either. Thus it can sometimes be difficult when faced with hormonal symptoms to discern whether the problem is with the direct producer of the hormone or with the pituitary, which controls the other glands. This is most often seen in difficult cases of infertility, hormonal imbalances and chronic fatigue.

Unfortunately, despite its protected location within the sella turçica, the pituitary can become damaged through various means. It can become enlarged or inflamed in connection with pregnancy and delivery of a baby, or the bones in the head (particularly the sphenoid bone) may for some reason create pressure on the turça sellica. It's always a good idea to first see a craniopath, generally a chiropractor or massage therapist who has specialized in moving cranial bones, whenever there is any question of a pituitary problem.

But it has recently come to light that the pituitary and/or the hypophysial stalk that connects it to the hypothalamus may also be prone to damage from all sorts of accidents dating back even to infancy, with significant lifelong consequences. Damage may arise from, for example, birth trauma (including the use of forceps), a Caesarian birth, or from shaken baby syndrome. Later causes might include a fall from a tree or a bunk bed, a car accident, sports injury or any number of other things with effects not immediately noticed.

Some symptoms of pituitary damage include:

- High blood pressure
- Gigantism
- Dwarfism
- Difficult pregnancies
- Lactation problems
- Low sex hormones
- Low thyroid function
- Low metabolism
- Water retention
- Temperature regulation
- Dysmenorrhea
- Weakness
- Poor memory
- Adrenal insufficiency
- Weight problems
- Hypoglycemia

Sometimes instead of functioning normally the pituitary will produce adenomas, which are hormone-filled sacs, leading to symptoms that mimic hypothyroidism. The symptoms of an adenoma can develop slowly, beginning, perhaps, with slight hormone imbalances or slight fatigue, but as the sac or adenoma grows the symptoms worsen, leading in time to severe frontal or migraine headaches and fatigue that worsens to the point of exhaustion and the need to sleep 12-15 hours a day. **(zzzz)** If a person has daily, severe headaches, especially frontal and between the eyes, or semihemiplegic migraines (pain, numbness, a burning sensation or paralysis on one side of the body), he or she should go to a doctor to be checked for an adenoma of the pituitary gland. A pituitary adenoma may be reduced by simply using Ultra Young Plus spray.

### The first step in taming your dragon:

*If you should have any hypo-pituitary condition, whether or not an adenoma is involved, use the Ultra Young Plus spray. It is best to spray it twice into each cheek four times a day. Use the spray for four months to make sure that the pituitary gland is balanced and functioning correctly again. It also helps to put a drop of Frankincense and a drop of Lavender oil on the roof of the mouth 4-5 times a day. For stronger action, substitute Sacred Frankincense and Idaho Balsam Fir. Some people still like to add raw pituitary glandular as it has building blocks to feed the pituitary and assist it in healing. And, of course, due to the high lipid content in the brain (the pituitary being part of the brain, of course), Omega Blues* **(dragons do love fish!)** *are a great* *supplement to these oils, providing as it does vital essential fatty acids.* (big aaah)

As a matter of possible interest, gigantism and dwarfism both stem from abnormalities in the pituitary production of HGH. I have used Ultra Young Plus spray for both conditions and have seen wonderful results.

## The Thyroid
Dragons have voracious appetites. This is why.

Under the direction of the pituitary, the thyroid secretes hormones, primarily thyroxin, that boost the metabolism of virtually every cell in the body, approximately doubling the body's rate of metabolic activity. A slow metabolism can cause weight gain while a fast metabolism may cause excess hunger. (Stomach rumbling) This effect extends to the other endocrine glands; thus if the thyroid doesn't send out the correct amount of thyroxin, the other endocrine glands won't be stimulated to produce their hormones properly. The thyroid may malfunction in being either under- or over-active. The more common condition is an under-active thyroid, called hypothyroidism.

Hypothyroidism is one cause of chronic fatigue syndrome. When the thyroid is underactive it can cause such profound fatigue that the sufferer simply does not want to get out of bed and do anything. The beginning stages of hypothyroidism may be characterized by mild fatigue, but as the condition worsens the person gets more and more tired each day. Many people complain of major depression or mental issues, not realizing that they have hypothyroidism, and after a visit to a medical doctor end up spending the rest of their lives on anti-depressant medications. Some people have said that they feel like they are living in a box in their head, screaming to get out of it. **(Help! Get me out of this cave!!!)** They feel like banging their head on a wall to relieve the pressure in the head. This is a sign that they may have not only hypothyroidism but a problem with the pituitary gland as well.

Symptoms of hypothyroidism include:
- Fatigue
- Weakness
- Weight gain or increased difficulty losing weight **(dragons can get fat you know!)**
- Coarse, dry hair
- Dry, rough pale skin
- Hair loss
- Cold intolerance (can't tolerate the cold like most people in the same environment) **(Dragons like to be hot!)**
- Muscle cramps and frequent muscle aches
- Constipation
- Depression
- Irritability
- Memory loss
- Abnormal menstrual cycles
- Decreased libido
- Hormonal imbalances

These symptoms may or may not all be present. Some may be milder than others. Sometimes a blood test will indicate hypothyroidism, while other times the test will come back within the "normal" range. But for you the problem is nonetheless real! How can that be? This is something well worth knowing, for your peace of mind.

The secret is that what is considered normal on lab tests derives from a bell-curve average of the local population as a whole. If your results fall within that range, you are considered to be healthy and your complaint is called "sub-clinical" – in other words, not worth worrying about (maybe even "all in your head"). But your personal normal health parameters in any particular area may fall outside the average, or it may take only a slight deviation, rather than a large one, from what is normal for you to cause significant problems. Unfortunately, conventional Western medicine relies on population averages as guidelines and does not address conditions regarded as sub-clinical. This is where alternative medicine comes to the rescue.

There are many different potential causes of hypothyroidism, including inflammation, nodules, and hypo-pituitarism, but hypothyroidism is fairly easy to treat.

### Dragon Taming step two:

*The first thing to do for a thyroid problem is to "jumpstart" Endoflex oil. The thyroid also loves Myrtle oil. Myrtle oil is found in Endoflex but sometimes it may be necessary to use more Myrtle in addition to the Endoflex. In addition to taking these oils orally, it is also helpful to rub Endoflex, Lemongrass and Myrtle on the throat. Sometimes people react to Lemongrass and break out in a rash on the throat where it was applied. You could try diluting it to see if you are sensitive that way. Do not put Lemongrass oil directly in the mouth undiluted. It is very hot and will burn and blister the mucosal lining of the mouth.*

*Thyromin is an excellent supplement to feed the thyroid whether it is under- or over-active, because it works to normalize the gland. Take two Thyromin capsules in the evening. Some people have found that taking Thyromin at night causes them to have insomnia for a few days. This passes in about 5 days. You can try taking one capsule for a few days and then move up to two, or try taking it in the morning for a week or two then switching back to night.*

The reason it is preferable to take the Thyromin in the evening is because the thyroid receives its major energy from the meridian system between 9 and 11 pm, so taking it then allows the body to use it at the proper time. But it is more important to take it at whatever time you can than to neglect to do so because of time constraints. Remember that it takes about four months to change a tissue in the body so do not stop doing your program before that time. You may or may not see quick results. If you do begin to feel better, you must still continue the program for the full four months to make sure that you do not backslide and that the tissues have truly healed. If you do not see immediate improvement, don't be discouraged; it may take the entire four months before you see any results.

Sometimes a person has adrenal insufficiency (see below) in addition to hypothyroidism. In this case, take two Thyromin in the evening and one in the morning. If you are utterly exhausted, keep adding one Thyromin in the evening, then one in the morning until you reach a level where your energy rises.

Besides hypothyroidism, a goiter can sometimes cause hyperthyroidism, which speeds up the body metabolism. A goiter shows up as a swelling around the thyroid. Other things can also cause swelling of the thyroid so it is best to have it checked out by a doctor.

A hypothyroid goiter is caused by not getting or absorbing enough iodine, the thyroid swelling in response as it tries to carry out its duties. *If you have been diagnosed with goiter, a simple test to see whether you need more iodine is to get some liquid iodine and paint a 2" square patch of your abdomen with it. Check it in 20 minutes. If it has absorbed into the skin and not left a stain, that is an indication that you need more iodine in your system. Repaint an area with iodine every day and check to see if there is a stain. If not, repaint with iodine the next day. When your body has all the iodine it needs, the painted iodine will not be absorbed but will instead stain the skin yellow or orange. Generally by then the goiter has disappeared. Most people begin staining within a few days, though some may take several weeks to get enough iodine into the system.*

In addition to simply not getting enough iodine in the diet, an iodine insufficiency can result from environmental factors, the most common being chemical pollutants added intentionally to our lives. Fluoride and chlorine from public water supplies and fluoride in toothpaste compete with iodine for the reception sites of the thyroid gland. This occurs because they are all halogens, members of group 17 on the periodic table of elements—but iodine is much less reactive than the other halogens. (Fluorine, in fact, is the most reactive of all elements.) That means that fluorine and chlorine bind more powerfully than iodine with the same elements or compounds. In the thyroid gland they latch onto the iodine receptor sites, but although they are chemically related to iodine, fluorine and chlorine do not perform any useful function in the thyroid gland. All they do is make it impossible for the thyroid to get the iodine it requires. I highly recommend that you get a good filter for your household water supply that will remove the fluorine and the chlorine. Regrettably, this isn't a problem with drinking water alone; these gases can also absorb through the skin in bath water.

Use a natural toothpaste that is fluoride-free. Despite whatever you may have been taught by the fluoridated-toothpaste industry, fluoride is not necessary for teeth or other bones, and in fact causes a whole host of health problems including mottled teeth, brittle bones, increased prevalence of hip fractures among the elderly and kidney stones. Toothpaste tubes even carry a warning not to swallow toothpaste, and to call the poison control center if you do. (By the way, sodium fluoride used to be the main ingredient in rat poison.) So if it's dangerous to swallow it, why put it in your mouth, where it is absorbed much more readily than it is in the digestive tract? Use a toothpaste that isn't contaminated with toxic fluoride. Dentrome, Dentrome Ultra and Dentrome Plus from Young Living Essential Oils are free of fluoride and contain essential oils that will kill undesirable microorganisms. You can also use soda and peroxide to clean your teeth safely.

## The Adrenal Glands

*A dragon may sometimes be draggin' and sometimes on a rampage. Stress!*

The adrenals are very busy glands, producing a whole host of hormones that play a large role in the regulation of body systems. Probably the most well-known is "adrenalin," more properly known as epinephrine. Adrenalin is what gives the body the energy to "get up and go." It is called the "fight or flight" hormone because the adrenals pump out a lot of it in emergency situations to increase the heart rate, inhibit the activity of the gastrointestinal tract and otherwise prime the body for action. **(Fire breathing roar! Whoosh and flapping of wings!)** Adrenalin also helps to control blood pressure, sweating, and other activities. (These are also co-regulated by the sympathetic nervous system.) This hormone is produced in the adrenal medulla along with norepinephrine, which works with epinephrine, and dopamine.

The cortex of the adrenal gland produces hormone building blocks for the reproductive system to create the male and female reproductive hormones. The adrenals also make some reproductive hormones themselves. Whenever there is any kind of trouble with hormones it is vital to include support for the adrenals in the treatment plan.

Additionally, the adrenal cortex produces adrenocorticoid hormones. These include various mineralocorticoids, mostly aldosterone, and glucocorticoids, the most well-known of which is cortisol. The primary role of aldosterone is to promote retention of sodium in the body, which causes retention of water. Without aldosterone we would quickly die of dehydration.

Cortisol is the "stress hormone." It is released under any type of stress. Its main purpose is to break down protein stores to allow the liver to turn protein into glucose rapidly so the brain can have more energy to deal with the stressful situation. The flight or flight mechanism in the body is working on high during times of stress and more energy and blood sugar is consumed. Elevated cortisol levels for any length of time can also begin to tear up ligaments between bones causing the spine to go out of alignment and joints to go out of juxtaposition easily and frequently. Further, cortisol can draw protein from the bones, leading to osteoporosis. In fact, cortisol causes the body to scavenge protein from everywhere (except the liver), breaking down everything for the sake of glucose for brainpower to deal with the perceived stress. It is also important to recognize that cortisol severely depresses the immune system.

Here are a few examples of stressors that could cause elevated levels of cortisol:

- Excess heat or cold
- Alcohol abuse
- Coffee drinking
- Depression
- Anxiety
- Malnutrition
- Personal relationships
- Physical or emotional trauma

- Surgery
- Job-related problems
- Diseases

The adrenal glands of a person who lives a stress-filled life are constantly secreting cortisol in an effort to deal with the stress, thereby tearing down muscles and bones and depressing the immune system. This person probably is also living in a constant state of fear (perhaps unrecognized), causing an over-production of adrenalin, which raises blood pressure and puts a strain on the heart. This condition of essentially being always "on alert" will wear a person out before their time, which effect is further exacerbated by the concomitant inhibitions of the digestive tract and the immune system.

The adrenals require a plentiful supply of minerals and B vitamins (especially B-6) at all times, but especially in the stressful conditions in which so many of us find ourselves these days. Without these building blocks, the adrenal glands may give a spike of hormones creating a feeling of energy followed closely by extreme fatigue because they cannot keep up with the job or have run out of materials to work with. People with hypoadrenia (adrenal insufficiency) will get up feeling fine in the morning but when they contemplate their morning work, or perhaps while in the middle of a job, they will suddenly get extremely tired.

Sometimes even the thought of work wears them out. For these people, any stress—whether physical, mental, emotional, financial or from whatever source—will cause the adrenal glands to either over-react and make the body either extremely tense or nervous, or else fail to respond, leaving them suddenly and extremely tired. **(snore, snort, snore)**

Nutmeg and Clove oils have corticosteroid activity. They are vital as supplements because they support the adrenal glands and help them to heal. Clove is too hot to take by mouth but can be used on the adrenal points of the feet. Nutmeg can be "jump-started" and used as needed. If you take Nutmeg oil, B-vitamins and minerals religiously, the hypoadrenia will turn itself around.

Some doctors put hypoadrenia patients on an adrenal glandular. There are different theories with regard to glandulars and how they work. One is that they have all the proper nutrients necessary to bring the adrenals back to health since they are chopped up and freeze-dried bovine or ovine adrenals. Another is that the hormones they contain will do the job of the adrenals, creating feedback to the pituitary to stop mandating the creation of more adrenal hormones, thus allowing the adrenal glands to rest and heal. A third theory is that whatever is attacking the adrenal glands will attack them (the glandulars), reducing the pressure on the adrenal glands so they can heal.

Sadly, I have personally known patients who had been on adrenal glandulars for a number of years and never healed, although their adrenal function was improved. When they started taking Nutmeg oil by mouth every day they were able to get off the glandulars and felt better than they had in years. Sometimes I have put a patient who is extremely fatigued on a glandular while at the same time supporting the adrenals with the proper essential oils so that the patient can have the strength and energy needed to get up and get going. Thyromin (for the thyroid) will also help the adrenal glands if taken in the morning.

When the body has too much cortisol, even minor stress can seem overwhelming to a person. In this case we give Cortistop to be used as directed on the bottle. Cortistop calms the body down and lowers the cortisol level. The patient begins to have more strength and energy as cortisol declines to a more normal level.

Recent studies have shown that drinking even 2-3 cups of coffee per day can raise cortisol levels. Depression, anxiety, panic disorder, malnutrition and alcohol abuse can also lead to elevated cortisol levels.

Adrenal insufficiency can also cause diabetes insipidus. This is a salt-handling problem that has symptoms similar to those of diabetes mellitus. The primary symptom is thirst. It seems that you can drink constantly and still not quench your thirst. Sometimes just increasing your potassium or trace minerals helps this problem. But sometimes the problem is that the cells aren't taking up the water and it is stored somewhere in the body instead of being utilized. Geranium oil corrects this problem by helping the cells take up water. Start by adding a drop of Geranium oil to each class of water that you drink in a day (and you should be drinking mostly water). You can eventually decrease this to a few drops a day. Once your water-handling problem begins to come under control, don't quit too soon or you will slide back to the original problem. Remember, it takes four months to heal a tissue.

According to research studies, adrenal insufficiency may be an underlying factor in hypoglycemia. It is also one of the causes of chronic fatigue.

On occasion I have found women who have both hypothyroidism and hypoadrenia. Upon further investigation, I usually discover that they also have a low estrogen level. After putting them on both Progessence cream and Sclaressence I find that they recover from their chronic fatigue, hypothyroidism and adrenal insufficiency almost overnight.

As was brought out in the section on the pituitary, damage to that gland can lead to symptoms of hypoadrenia, yet treatment of the adrenals would not resolve the condition. Hypo-pituitarism must always be ruled out first. Addison's disease can also result from hypoadrenia and this too may stem from an underlying state of hypo-pituitarism.

### Dragon Taming Step 3

*Again, to feed the adrenals every day one must take Super B, Omega Blues,* **(there's that fish again)** *and Trace Minerals. Essential Oils support the adrenals glands also. The best ones being Clove, Nutmeg, Endoflex and En-R-Gee.*

**Estrogen and Progesterone**
If not in balance, this is where the fire starts

When we speak of women's hormones, we are referring primarily to estrogen and progesterone. Generally speaking, the majority of women have an excess of estrogen and a serious deficiency of progesterone.

I want to address the role of progesterone first. A woman needs progesterone to get pregnant and stay pregnant. (It promotes gestation.) If the progesterone level in the body is too low, either the ovaries will not release their eggs or the egg when fertilized cannot attach correctly to the lining of the uterus. A natural progesterone cream such as Progessence or Progessence Plus Serum from Young Living may help boost progesterone to normal levels.

Progesterone is produced in the ovaries (in the corpus luteum, following ovulation), the adrenal glands and, during pregnancy, in the placenta. Progesterone is also stored in adipose (fat) tissue.

Let me explain why progesterone is so critically important in the female body, even for women who are menopausal, or don't have periods, or who even have had a hysterectomy. **(Yes, dragons can live to a ripe old age.)** Exciting discoveries have recently shown that progesterone is necessary for all women and even some young girls, because there are hormone receptors on individual cells, maybe all cells, throughout the body, acting as gateways for progesterone to enter the cell. This is especially true for "female" areas of the body. Progesterone is also a neurosteroid, meaning that it is produced and used in the nervous system in addition to the reproductive system.

It has been found that neurosteroids such as progesterone affect the synaptic functioning and the myelination of the nerves – in other words, the ability of nerves to carry signals. And progesterone is a significant actor in the brain. As a matter of fact one study found that fully a third of the women who have epileptic seizures had low levels of progesterone. Epileptic drugs didn't help control their seizures but an increase of progesterone did. Progesterone may also play an important role in memory and cognitive ability, raising the possibility that some women with Alzheimer's may simply have low levels of progesterone. In addition, progesterone is a bipolar mood stabilizer and, as such, might be a great replacement for anti-depressants. (I am not telling anyone to go ahead and get off their anti-depressant medication.)

Progesterone is called a sex hormone not because it increases sexual pleasure or plays a role in reproduction, but because it is prominent in the female gender. Yes, even women over 60 do still need progesterone. Females need progesterone without regard to their reproductive status; it's part of their female nature.

Turning now to the reproductive system, though, we find that after birth the body suddenly goes from a high estrogen state, which was necessary for delivery, to a more balanced state. Failure to increase the level of progesterone can lead to post-partum blues and also low milk supply. I am aware that some doctors say that progesterone as well as estrogen must drop to a low level after delivery, but my experience says that women often need more progesterone. Progesterone supplementation will not harm the baby, before or after birth, and in fact is critical to the health of the embryo. (This is an important argument against so-called "emergency contraceptive" pills – if there is already a developing embryo the pills will deprive it of the progesterone it has to have.) Progesterone also just might increase your milk supply. The breast is full of progesterone receptors!

I want to say a little bit about progesterone receptors. As noted above, a receptor is a gateway for something to enter the cell. It is protein based. It needs what is called a ligand to hold the hormone or the mineral or other nutrient to enter the cell. In the case of progesterone receptors, first estrogen has to attach to the receptor. Then progesterone attaches to the estrogen. Then the chemical reaction can take place in the cell that the hormones were sent to start. If progesterone isn't there, the estrogen will inhibit the chemical process, and if it stays there long enough without progesterone attaching, it can incite the cell to mutate, causing cancer or tumors. This is why progesterone has to "oppose" or "contest" estrogen. It means they have to work together! It isn't one or the other in the body at once; it is both at the same time, in proper balance.

*An exciting new product from Young Living called Progessence Plus has proven very helpful in boosting progesterone levels and bringing estrogen and progesterone into balance. It has already made a huge difference in many women's lives. Please learn about it beginning on page 38.* (Tail wagging and thumping)

Now let's turn to the subject of estrogen. Estrogen is just as vital for a woman as progesterone, but the tendency among American women nowadays is toward a state of excess estrogen, so it has acquired a reputation as a troublemaker.

Estrogen is responsible for "feminizing" women's bodies, for preparing the uterus for pregnancy, for maintaining skin, blood vessels and bones as well as genitourinary tissues and for various other functions throughout the body, including memory. It also increases fat storage and water retention. (bloop)

At elevated levels, estrogen exaggerates its normal effects by, for example, making you too fat, or making lumpy or fibrocystic breasts or even causing breast cancer. (The great majority of breast cancers need estrogen to grow.) It makes you crave sweets. It can cause migraines and insomnia, weaken libido, inhibit orgasm and depress the thyroid (leading to tiredness and a lack of energy), and it can promote nervousness and jitters. And if that weren't enough, it stores in body fat.

Well, the question is why people nowadays have excessive amounts of estrogen. A significant reason comes from outside the endocrine system. An unfortunate fact of modern life is our constant exposure to xenoestrogens in our food and in our environment. Though derived from petroleum in laboratories, they are similar enough in structure to human estrogen to interfere with normal biological functions. Petroleum is not alive, and things made from petroleum are not alive, so why would we want them contaminating our bodies?

Xenoestrogens are present in some food additives, hormones fed to animals that we later eat, insecticides, weed killers, plastics, shampoo, linings of food and drink cans, cosmetics, detergents and a host of other chemicals. Hormone replacement treatments and oral contraceptives made from horse urine are another class of xenoestrogens. Being fat-soluble like natural estrogens and steroids, xenoestrogens are readily stored in fatty tissues in the body.

Following their original use for whatever purpose, xenoestrogens typically end up polluting our water, where they are picked up by fish and wildlife – and people. This includes that portion of the food additives and contraceptives (and other pharmaceuticals) we ingest and don't metabolize. Thus almost everyone is exposed to these artificial substances "the second time around," even if conscientiously trying to avoid using them.

Xenoestrogens can attach to the estrogen receptor sites on cells, causing tumor formation and preventing progesterone from being able to attach properly. Xenoestrogens also directly impact the reproductive system (in males as well as females) and probably the developing fetus. Obviously, it is vitally important to avoid them in our food and in our environment and to cleanse the body of toxins.

In the breast, xenoestrogens (like natural estrogens) cause cell division, enlarging the breasts. Too many xenoestrogens mean that when the pituitary sends out its monthly signal to increase estrogen, helping prepare the breasts for lactation, excessive cell division can cause lumps, fibrocystic disease or cancer. If you have a history of estrogen-related cancers (xenoestrogens have been implicated in ovarian cancer as well as breast cancer) it is crucial to take progesterone supplements to assist the body in clearing those toxins.

There are also, in addition to xenoestrogens, things called phytoestrogens, which are made by plants and are, like xenoestrogens, structurally similar to the estrogen our human bodies make. Phytoestrogens are found mainly in grains, soy foods and fruits and vegetables. **(YEAH! Bring on the food!)** The good news is that they don't seem to cause the health problems that xenoestrogens do, and in fact may be quite beneficial. Some studies indicate that women who eat a lot of foods containing phytoestrogens have a reduced incidence of breast cancer, and also that they eliminate more estrogens in their urine. In the event a person has difficulty digesting cabbage, broccoli, soyfoods or other foods that contain high quantities of phytoestrogens, the problem in all likelihood lies not with the foods themselves but with the digestive system, most probably the liver. Cleanse the liver and be healthy! *See my book "Inner Transformations Using Essential Oils."*

The problem then, is what to do about all the xenoestrogens to which we are exposed constantly. Clearly, the first step is to avoid them as much as possible. Avoid eating food out of plastic containers, and by all means, do not microwave food in plastic. (I prefer fresh and raw anyway.) Xenoestrogens are found in the lining of almost all food cans in the U.S. as well as in plastic bottles of types 3 and 7 (stamped on the bottom) and things made of polycarbonate plastic. Stay away from weed killers that contain atrazine, and most insecticides. Be careful with thermal paper receipts and carbonless copy paper. Watch out for propyl gallate, used as an antioxidant in food products. These are just a few of the sources of xenoestrogens in our everyday environment.

Second, we can eat a healthy diet low in refined, processed carbohydrates and sugars and high in fresh vegetables such as broccoli, spinach and green leafy vegetables in general. These are high in phytoestrogens that may help draw down excess estrogens in the body. Remember to wash fresh vegetables and fruits to remove pesticides.

Third, we can use a whole-house water filter to try to remove them from our water. Public water treatment plants do not remove them.

Fourth, we can use progesterone supplements to balance and remove them from our bodies. Progesterone can not only restore balance but can also coax excess estrogens and xenoestrogens from fatty tissue. When both are present in excess, the liver will get rid of them. Progessence Plus serum is the most effective progesterone supplement I have seen.

Finally, it would be an excellent idea to establish an annual routine of cleansing your colon and liver followed by a Master Cleanse. *(Instructions for all these are in Inner Transformations Using Essential Oils.)*

An added benefit of taking progesterone as a supplement is that it can break down to more basic steroid hormones and attach to androgen receptor sites as either androgen or progesterone causing those sites to be able to carry out their biological processes. These sites include critical anti-inflammatory receptors, energy making receptors, blood pressure regulators etc.

Here are more things that progesterone does:
- It raises epidermal growth factor-1 levels, a factor often used to induce proliferation, and used to sustain cultures, of stem cells.
- It increases core temperature (thermogenic function) during ovulation.
- It reduces spasm and relaxes smooth muscle. Bronchi are widened and mucus regulated. (Progesterone receptors are widely present in submucosal tissue.)
- It acts as an anti-inflammatory agent and regulates the immune response.
- It reduces gall-bladder activity.
- It normalizes blood clotting and vascular tone, zinc and copper levels, cell oxygen levels, and use of fat stores for energy.
- It may affect gum health, decreasing risk of gingivitis (gum inflammation) and tooth decay.
- It appears to prevent endometrial cancer (involving the uterine lining) by regulating the effects of estrogen.

Symptoms and problems associated with low progesterone/estrogen dominance include:

- Tender Breasts
- Mood Swings (PMS) **(growl)**
- Water Retention
- Weepiness
- Cyclical headaches-migraines
- Low Libido
- Irritability & quick to anger **(roar)**
- Anxiety
- Uterine Fibroids
- Puffiness and Bloating
- Bleeding Changes
- Cold Body Temperature
- Cystic Ovaries-Polycystic Ovary
- Vaginitis and vaginal infections
- Dry vagina little mucus
- Uterine or endometrial cancer
- Fungal or Candida Infections
- Heavy menses
- Breast cancer
- Sleep disturbances
- Sugar cravings
- Elevated Triglycerides
- Infertility
- Variations in menstrual cycle
- Leaky bladder
- Interstitial cystitis
- Tingling of hands and feet, possibly even trigeminal neuralgia and tinnitus
- Fibromyalgia,
- Leaky bladder
- Digestion problems
- Low blood sugar

Obviously, excess estrogen (whether produced in the body or, more likely, from the laboratory) is a significant threat to women's health. But estrogen is not a bad hormone; on the contrary, it is vital in proper amounts. Estrogen and progesterone, in balance, make for a happy woman.

Some women suffer from low estrogen and at the same time even lower progesterone. Both of these conditions may be improved by using Progessence, especially Progessence Plus. If the body is low on estrogen, or was only lacking estrogen to begin with, a pregnenolone cream used either instead of progesterone or in conjunction with it and used in the same way may help the body. Pregnenolone is the precursor to most hormones, meaning that it is the building block from which most hormones are made. The endocrine glands will take the basic pregnenolone ring molecule and add other molecules to produce their own respective hormones. Prenolone cream from Young Living Essential Oils is a natural pregnenolone cream, while Progessence is specifically a progesterone cream that also includes essential oils and other helpful ingredients. In my many years of assisting women with hormonal difficulties we have had the best results using creams from Young Living.

Also important are colon cleansing and support for the pituitary, thyroid and adrenal.

## Infertility
### How to hatch dragon eggs

Infertility is becoming pandemic in the U.S. Ironically, in our abortion-plagued nation there are innumerable women who want children but can't get pregnant despite all the efforts of medical science. I have found in my practice that most women who cannot get pregnant have problems with their bowel and liver functions. This may seem odd at first until we realize that stagnant bowels send toxins into the uterus and a malfunctioning liver causes a hormonal imbalance. For the majority of women, doing colon and liver cleanses helps correct the problem and allows them to get pregnant. It's almost miraculous. I personally have assisted hundreds of women to become pregnant by teaching them sound cleansing principles. Most have gotten pregnant within 3-6 months of doing a colon cleanse followed by a liver cleanse. If a patient was not pregnant within 6 months of starting these cleanses, we looked at other factors such as thyroid and adrenal insufficiencies. Out of all the women that I worked with only five did not get pregnant after doing the cleanses. These five women were all sisters and had emotional issues that they were not ready to deal with at the time.

An article in London's Daily Times discussed the cost of infertility. It said that it typically took at least four infertility treatments at $25,000 a session to impregnate a woman. That would add up to $100,000—and even then only a quarter of the women treated succeeded in becoming pregnant. This article went on to say that it was worthwhile for the British medical system to pay for the treatments because each child would, over its lifetime, pay the government back in the amount of taxes that they paid. That seems a little callous to me. Another article from the New York Times talked about the threat of a declining tax base resulting from the American population just barely being able to replace itself. However, the article did mention at the very end the most important reason to have children, which is pure joy. It is tragic that so many husbands and wives wish to have children and are unable to, when the answer can be as simple as cleaning up the body's systems so that each organ can work at its optimal level.

Modern Western medicine typically looks only at the reproductive system in cases of infertility. Medical doctors have forgotten the importance of the liver's role as a major hormone balancer. One of its many jobs is to destroy excess "used" hormones so that there aren't too many floating in the bloodstream, which would cause the hypothalamus to fail to signal the pituitary gland to send out fresh hormones. If there are too many hormones in the body it becomes unbalanced and symptomatic. For example, an excess of estrogen might lead a woman to experience hot flashes, bouts of anger or depression, weight gain, cramps or irregular cycles.

Another important factor in the body's capacity to make hormones is the liver's ability to process fatty acids. We must have fats in the diet to make steroid hormones, and the liver has to be able to process them. Lipozyme taken with a meal helps digest fatty acids so they can be used as hormone building blocks. It may be, in our low-fat-obsessed diet industry, that some people don't get enough healthful fats in their foods to supply the building blocks for steroid hormones. Taking essential fatty acids as found in such supplements as flaxseed oil, evening primrose oil and fish oils helps supply the correct type of fatty acids with which to make these hormones. Avoid trans fats; they are unnatural substances typically encountered as hydrogenated or partially-hydrogenated vegetable oils. They interfere with normal metabolism and do not provide the building blocks for hormone creation.

Other problems hindering fertility originate within the digestive tract itself. First, if the stomach isn't digesting proteins or the small intestine isn't producing the proper enzymes or absorption of fats is not occurring for some reason, the reproductive system will not receive the proper nourishment and the necessary constituents for the vital proteins and hormones will not be available. Secondly, lack of vitality in the colon could prevent pregnancy. If the colon is sluggish or clogged, toxins can leach from it into the nearby tissues of the reproductive system, e.g. the uterus, and contaminate them so that they can't function properly.

The good news is that it usually only takes 3-6 months of colon and liver cleansing for a woman to be restored to fertility.

I saw a particular case where a woman had had two children following which her period stopped for 11 years. Within three months of doing a colon and liver cleanse, her period started up again. A month later, she was pregnant.

Unfortunately she miscarried that baby. But two months later, she became pregnant again. She carried that baby, a little girl, full term. When I last spoke to her and her husband, they had had three more children and were so grateful that I had taught them the principles of colon and liver health so her body could function better.

## How to Use Essential Oils for Hormonal Problems
### Taming your dragon step 4

Essential oils are homeostatic, meaning that they bring balance to the body. This is a crucial difference between essential oils and pharmaceuticals. Essential oils do not force change on the body, they simply promote a healthful state.

Some essential oils evoke a hormone-like response in the body. Some essential oils will act like estrogen at one time and at other times act like progesterone, depending on what your body needs at the time. So in other words, the oils don't stimulate estrogen unless you need it to be stimulated. Many oils are described as having emmenagogic or menstrual cycle-regulating effects; these include Clary Sage, Rose, Jasmine, Juniper, Sweet Fennel, Cedarwood, Sweet Marjoram, Rosemary, Peppermint, Anise Basil, Angelica Root, Cypress, Sage, Lavender And Ylang Ylang. Their menstrual-regulating effects come not by adding sex hormone-like compounds to the body but by stimulating and or/decreasing the production of follicle stimulation and lutenizing hormone by anterior pituitary with its consequent effects on the menstrual cycle. Therefore they stimulate the gut, uterus, adrenals and ovaries to produce more hormones depending on what the body needs at that time.

## Progessence Plus

Before discussing how to use other essential oils for woman-specific problems, I would like to first talk about a wonderful new product from Young Living called Progessence Plus. I feel that using Progessence Plus serum is one of the most health-promoting things that a women can do for her body. Progessence Plus is micronized human bio-identical progesterone derived from wild yam in a base of vitamin E derived from palm oil. It also contains copaiba, frankincense, bergamot, clove and peppermint in it to assist it to enter the cell more easily and for additional benefits. Because it goes into the cell so quickly it is very potent. We have already discussed the critical roles that progesterone plays in the female body, so it is obvious that taking Progessence Plus will provide huge benefits.

Progessence Plus is essential for every woman, especially if she has ever suffered pituitary damage. It works wonderfully for teenagers who have cramps or headaches during their periods: just a couple of drops usually takes care of their problem. It is especially important for women of menopausal age since their bodies still need progesterone but are producing so little of it. Women continue to make estrogen in the lining of the gut and in the adrenals after menopause, and thus become estrogen dominant, especially with the added xenoestrogens we get from our environment. So you need progesterone to balance the estrogen.

Progessence Plus is safe to take during pregnancy, and indispensable for women who have a history of miscarriage, since low progesterone is the number one cause of miscarriage. It is safe to take while breast feeding and even while breast feeding baby boys. It may even increase your milk supply.

Women who have had breast cancer or who have a family history of breast cancer should take Progessence Plus to increase the progesterone in their body to be able to balance estrogen dominancy (remember, most breast cancers depend on estrogen for growth). It may not be a good idea to take Progessence Plus if you are on birth control pills or HRT. You may want to consult with a medical doctor who is familiar with bio-identical micronized progesterone if you are on any type of medications including thyroid medicines.

Note that Progessence is definitely not for men. It reportedly lowers libido and tends to inflame vascular endothelium which could lead to strokes and heart attacks.

Just as there are many different kinds of dragons, each of us is a unique individual and each of us will use Progessence Plus in a different way. My dragon is hot and very thirsty, he seems to come out roaring once a month wanting sweets and breathing fire on all those around. How

I use Progessence Plus will be different than how someone else uses it. Perhaps your dragon is very cold and very sleepy, or extremely moody and weepy. Each woman's hormonal makeup is her own and can vary even day to day, so general guidelines are just that – general guidelines. Be aware of your own body and make adjustments as needed.

It is best to start slowly with Progessence Plus and to use it symptomatically. Use a drop or two at a time rubbing it lightly over the carotid artery (or any vein you can see). Use it for headaches, for moodiness, for anger, for depression, for cramps, for hot flashes, for food cravings etc. Just take it for any ill feeling during the day. I use it every two hours throughout the day for constant effectiveness.

There is an adjustment time for the progesterone to become balanced with other hormones in the body and to reach an optimum overall level. You may find yourself taking more of it on some days then you do on another. If your symptoms increase or you become nauseous, <u>take more</u> because that indicates that your progesterone levels are very low. You do not need to cycle Progessence Plus, in other words, you don't have to stop using it for the seven days that you are having your period like we were taught to do on progesterone creams. Since your body uses progesterone constantly it is important that you have some every day regardless of what your menstrual cycle is doing. Later in this booklet we will learn just which hormones are most needed on what day during a 28 day cycle.

Most women only need a drop or two a day rubbed onto the carotid artery. You may feel joy! Your libido may rise, your periods will be better, bleeding will not be as heavy. You may have an increase of energy. You may lose water weight or even fat. Incontinence disappears. Bowel and bladder function as well as digestion may improve. Throngs of women are enjoying amazing results from using Progessence plus. For some it happens quickly, but for many women these results happen over a period of several weeks or even months. It all depends on how depleted of progesterone or estrogen your body has become. It's okay either way; each of us is unique.

## Troubleshooting Progessence Plus

Here are a few ideas to assist you if you become symptomatic while on Progessence Plus. Please remember that if you run into troubles, chances are you need a lot more Progessence Plus and/or estrogen. Try using just a drop of Progessence Plus rubbed on your carotid artery area of the neck or on your wrist or elbow crease every minute to 5 minutes to see if the symptoms improve. You can get estrogen from either Estro or Femigen. So increase these things first. But if that approach doesn't work, experiment with the other supplements and ideas listed as follows.

**Severe headaches** (especially frontal)
Ultra Young Spray two sprays per cheek 5 times a day.
A drop of Frankincense and a drop of Idaho Balsam Fir rubbed in the roof of your mouth at the same time.

**Throat tightness**

Take 2 Thyromin at night and use Myrtle throughout the day on the throat.

**Brain fog**

Diffuse Frankincense several times a day. I like to go five minutes on and 15 minutes off.

**Starvation fits**

Immediately drink water, take a tsp of cod liver oil and drink a shot of NingXia Red. If you still feel hungry, grab some protein. Stay away from carbs or sugars as they could make you gain weight. The starvation feeling comes from the pituitary and pancreas readjusting to the added progesterone. The pancreas loves NingXia Red or any wolfberry product, so just do these steps and hang in there. It will settle down.

**Leaky bladder or increased urination**

Be glad, you are getting rid of excess water! If this continues for more than a few weeks, find a midwife who knows how to lift the uterus or colon off the bladder. There are exercises to strengthen the pelvic floor.

**Insomnia**

Increase your magnesium intake. Try Progessence Plus at night. Take Cortistop. Use Idaho Balsam Fir or Peace and Calming or Tranquil.

**Can't lose weight**

Be patient. It may take a few months before this happens for you. Your energy will increase, your ability to exercise will increase, and your appetite will normalize. Support your thyroid as above. Use ThermaBurn and grapefruit oil.

**Nausea or vomiting**

Take Estro, use Di-Gize or Peppermint. Sometimes even more Progessence helps. Be patient, this will disappear in about a week.

**Edema**

Because the Progessence Plus is acting as an anti-inflammatory, the exudates are being released into the lymph channels. Use Ledum and Grapefruit to thin it down and assist it to clear. It would help to go on a colon cleanse and liver cleanse to assist the body in dumping these toxins. Drinking lemon juice or VitaLife juice (beet, carrot, radish) helps to remove toxins from the body.

**Acne**

Toxins may be coming out of the skin, causing acne. Cleanse as above. It may also be that the liver isn't disposing of excess hormones, so cleanse the liver.

**Rashes**

Although Young Living does not recommend taking Progessence Plus serum by mouth, some people may not tolerate it on their skin because of sensitivity, or from a detoxification effect. As a result, some have taken it by mouth or experimented with various other application sites.

**Increased hot flashes**

Hold on, this will pass! Use Estro immediately, and put Peppermint on your feet, hands and spine. Try supporting the thyroid with Myrtle and Thyromin, and take Femigen.

**Hair loss**

Rarely, women may experience hair loss while taking Progessence Plus. I do not believe this is caused directly by the serum, but may occur as the increased progesterone in the body possibly causes the adrenals to perk up and use the body's store of essential fatty acids to bring all the steroid hormones into balance. The depletion of fatty acids in turn leads to hair loss. Other factors may include the liver not metabolizing proteins and fats, or thyroid or pituitary insufficiency.

**Mood swings and other symptoms**

If you find your mood changing during the day or if you get a dull headache during the day, use more Progessence Plus at that time. The serum may also help with painful periods, and with the cramps, heavy bleeding, water weight gain and constipation or diarrhea sometimes associated with periods.

**For the very worst cases**

A relatively small number of women experience what I call the bucking bronco ride. They suffer worsening symptoms of headache, acne, hot flashes and sudden onsets of starvation. They are hit with increased weight, increased water retention, horrible nausea or even vomiting. What is going on and how can we deal with this? First, I want to say, hold on! Keep riding! The problem is that your sex hormones are so low that they are kicking and bucking as they struggle to rise to a new and better level. You may even have low estrogen in addition to the usual low progesterone.

Let's go over some of the things that you can do to assist your body in coming back to balance. I believe the underlying cause of all this most likely is that long-term damage to the pituitary gland has kept your hormones suppressed, so you must take care of the pituitary as explained near the beginning of this booklet as well as following the advice in this section. Don't give up and go back to the state you were in.

Give yourself some time to heal and realize that the body is going to work on its highest priority for survival first, not what you subjectively think should be your highest priority (e.g., hot flashes!). Then it will go on to whatever is next on its list. To repeat: it might take several months to heal!

In your desire to get well quickly you may have started out taking a whole lot more Progessence Plus at a time than your particular body can handle. So don't begin with a lot at once. Your bronco ride will smooth out if you take just a drop or two of Progessence Plus at a time consistently throughout the day rather than taking it only once or twice. If they do, great! Stay with that amount until you find you can use more. If symptoms worsen, grab some Estro and take a dropperful or even up to three dropperfuls to balance out the Progessence Plus. Start taking two Femigen a day.

Feed your body the building blocks it needs to make more hormones and convert the Estro and Femigen into estrogen. The means give it essential fatty acids such as Omega Blues or cod liver oil. Use Prenolone cream so your body can have the base of all hormones available, or use PD80/20 for the same purpose. Make sure you are getting vitamin D. That can be done by simply being in the sun for 15 minutes a day. Give yourself trace minerals along with B vitamins such as found in Super B or True Source. All these additional supplements plus nutritional support for the pituitary, thyroid and adrenal will assist you in coming back into balance.

Patiently give yourself four months to effect a change and bring yourself back to balance. I personally saw a lot of welcome improvements in my own health in only one month's time, but again, each woman is one of a kind and it may take you the entire four months before you see a change. Don't give up!

## The Menstrual Cycle
## The dragon mood barometer

As we have learned, progesterone and estrogen play many roles in the day-to-day metabolic functions of the female body. Of course, these two hormones are most frequently encountered in connection with the menstrual cycle. The pituitary signals the release of these hormones in a specific pattern to mature an ovum and also to create a menstrual cycle.

An accurate understanding of the female cycle empowers us to keep track of what hormones are active each day so that if we encounter difficulties we will know what nutritional product or essential oil to use to clear up the problem. Therefore I have included a chart to show in graphic form what actually happens at each point in the cycle.

This is a chart showing what hormones are active during each day of the female cycle.

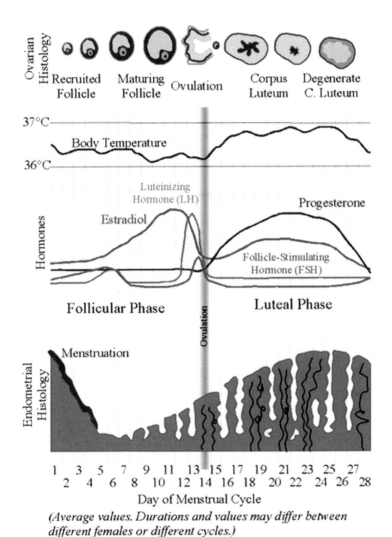

(Average values. Durations and values may differ between different females or different cycles.)

Starting on day one and looking at the bottom of the chart we see a mountain of red sloughing off. This is to represent what is happening to our endometrial lining. From day 1 to day 7 it sloughs off. Then from day 7 through 24 it builds up again before begins to slow down on day 21 and begins to break down then slough off again on day 28.

At the top of the chart we see that the egg is released on day 14 and then travels down the fallopian tube. By day 21 it should arrive in the uterus and if it has been fertilized it will implant itself on the endometrial lining. If it hasn't been fertilized by the time of its arrival it dissolves. If a fertilized egg does implant it secretes a hormone triggering the ovarian cyst that released it to continue to produce progesterone. If the ovary doesn't receive that signal the cyst dries up and stops producing the progesterone so that by day 28 the progesterone stops and the period begins.

**Day 1 to Day 14** is known at the follicular phase or estrogen phase.

Looking up at the graph of hormones, we see that starting on day 1 there is slightly more estrogen (blue line) than there is of the other hormones. That blue line begins to build about day 7 slowly coming to a peak around day 11 then sloping off sharply by day 14.

Estrogen is dominant during this phase but some progesterone (the black line on the graph) is still needed to balance the estrogen. On day 1 there is very little LH (luteinizing hormone), represented by the green line, and likewise very little FSH (follicle-stimulating hormone), as shown by the red line. There is a slight peak for both of these around day 5, followed by a much larger spike at day 13-14. Notice that LH, from the pituitary, peaks a half day to a full day earlier then FSH, from the thyroid. Then they decrease sharply to very little during the second half of the period.

**Day 14 to Day 28** is called the Luteal Phase or the Progesterone Phase

There is also a small amount of progesterone going forward from day one, but little or no LH or FSH. Progesterone is present at a low level until day 14, when it begins to build rapidly, reaching its peak at about day 22 and then falling back down to very little on day 28. Notice that estrogen is also being used during this part of the cycle but not to the same degree as during the first half of the menstrual cycle.

## Troubleshooting Menstrual Problems

The following products from Young Living Oils support the organs of the female cycle.

- Liver: *JuvaTone, JuvaCleanse, Release, Forgiveness*
- Adrenal: *Super B, Mineral Essence, Omega Blues, Nutmeg, Clove, Endoflex, Thyromin, Cortistop, Endogize, Prenolone cream*

- Pituitary Gland:   *Ultra Young Spray, Endogize, Frankincense, Cedarwood, Lavender*
- Thyroid:   *Thyromin, Endogize, Myrrh, Myrtle, Lemongrass, Endoflex*
- Ovaries:   *Progessence Cream, Progessence Plus*
- Uterus:   *Estro, Clary Sage, Sclaressence, Lady Sclarol, Dragon Time*

The following are some problems that arise from lack or excess of sex-related hormones and general guidelines for their treatment using Progessence Plus, Prenolone and other natural products. These, again, are general guidelines, because everyone's body is unique.

**Cycle longer than 28 days**

The most common problem when the menstrual period is off its normal 28 day cycle is that the follicular phase is longer than the luteal phase, not giving the ovum the correct timing to come down the fallopian tubes. The problem is generally that the signal from the pituitary gland is off a day or two. This could lead to periods that are too short (less than 28 days) or too long (more than 28 days).

This can be corrected by giving your body certain essential oils and nutrition each day that will assist the body in knowing what its timing is supposed to be.

Day 1
Today is the day that the period or menses should start.

Days 1-7
Support Uterus with a small amount of Clary Sage, Sclaressence, Lady Sclarol, or Dragon Time around the ankles once or twice a day. Take Progessence Plus as needed for headaches, mood swings, aches and pains or any other symptom of ill being.

Days 3-4
Support the pituitary and thyroid by taking a few sprays of Ultra Young + Spray during the day and a Thyromin or Endogize pill at night. You can also use the listed oils around the throat during these days. Continue using the Progessence Plus as needed.

Days 7-11
Ramp Clary Sage or its blends. By ramping, I mean to take a little more each day until you get to the peak on the chart. Continue using the Progessence Plus as needed.

Day 12
Stop taking Clary Sage or its blends. Continue using the Progessence Plus as needed.

Day 13
Spray a few Sprays of Ultra Young + Spray in the mouth throughout the day to support the pituitary gland. Continue using the Progessence Plus as needed.

Day 14

Take two Thyromin at night to support the thyroid. You may also want to use Myrrh, Myrtle, Lemongrass or Endoflex on the throat during this day. Continue using the Progessence Plus as needed.

Day 14

There is supposed to be a surge of testosterone on this day, so smell a little bit of Mister oil or Goldenrod oil and put some on your ankles. Continue using the Progessence Plus as needed.

Day 15

Start ramping Progessence Cream 15-25 mg daily. Start with 1/4 tsp per day and build to 1/2 tsp per day. You can take as much as 1 tsp a day if you need. Or you can just use Progessence Plus. You will find during this half of the cycle, you may need more Progessence Plus then you did the first half of the cycle.

Day 22

Begin decreasing Progessence Cream. Continue using the Progessence Plus as needed.

Day 28

Start over as if it is day 1 of your period. Decrease progesterone and increase Femigen and estrogenic oils. When your period starts count that as Day 1 again. It might take several months before your period becomes regular. Stop taking Progessence cream.

Please note that if you are using Progessence Plus you may not need to use Progessence cream. They can be used together and in so using the cream you may not need as much of the serum.

Repeat the cycle. It might take 3-6 months before your cycle straightens out and your period begins.

Take Super B and trace minerals and Omega Blues every day to support the adrenal gland. Also if you still don't have a normal period then increase the amount of Ultra Young + Spray and Thyromin you are using during the first half of the cycle. You may also want to take Prenolone Cream during the peaks of the cycle to support the adrenal gland to make more hormones. The Prenolone cream can be used during both halves of the cycle. If you are already using Ultra Young + Spray and Thyromin daily due to damaged Pituitary Gland then increase the amount that you use on days 3,4, and 10-13.

**Cycle shorter than 28 days**

Make sure that you are supporting the pituitary gland daily for four months. Use at least 2 drops of Progessence Plus daily or as needed. Use ½-1 tsp Prenolone Cream daily. As you go through the month make sure that you are using the essential oils that support each day. Take 2 Femigen daily. Do not stop until the cycle becomes more even. Make sure to support the adrenal gland. Increase the amount of Ultra Young + spray and Thyromin that you use on days 3, 4 and 10-13.

**Irregular periods**

Use Progessence Plus as above everyday as needed supporting it with Prenolone, Femigen, and Omega Blues. Counting the first day of your period as day one make sure that you use more Ultra Young + Spray and Thyromin on days 3, 4, and10- 13. Decrease the amount of Estrogenic oils on day 14. Take a few drops of Golden Rod or Testosterone on day 14 and 13. Increase the amount of Progessence Plus during the next 15 days. On day 28 start over as if it is day 1 of your period. Decrease progesterone and increase Femigen and Estrogenic Oils. When your period starts then start counting as if it is Day 1 again. It might take several months before your period becomes regular.

**Amenorrhea (No menstrual periods)**

Use the new moon cycle to help you know when and how much cream to use. For example, our menstrual periods, like the moon, should be on a 28-day cycle. The hormone progesterone increases toward the 14th day just as the moon waxes to full in 14 days. Then it decreases toward the 28th day. So call the new moon day 1. You probably have pituitary damage so make sure you are supporting the pituitary gland with Ultra Young + Spray and Frankincense and Idaho Balsam Fir. Take Progessence Plus daily and follow the advice given above for a typical cycle. When you get to day 28, start over with day one.

**Menopausal women (including those who have had partial or complete hysterectomies)**

It is extremely important that you of all women be taking Progessence Plus. You aren't making as much progesterone anymore in the ovaries but the lining of the gut and the adrenals are still pumping out estrogen. Further, the estrogen has been stored in your fat so you can have it on hand when your body stops making as much of it. Thus it is very important that you support the adrenal in its job of making progesterone by giving it the building blocks to make progesterone. These building blocks are found in Prenolone cream, Super B or True Source, Trace Minerals, and Omega Blues.

Use a couple of drops of Progessence Plus daily either on your neck on the backs of your hands. Balance with Femigen or Estro as described in the Troubleshooting section.

Since you don't want your periods to begin, you may start by just working the peak days like this:

On day 3-4 support the pituitary and thyroid with Ultra Young Spray and Thyromin as above.

On day 9 or 10 give yourself a little Clary Sage or Clary Sage products, building it up a little at a time until day 13. If you are getting angry or having hot flashes, stop the Clary Sage and add Progessence Plus to balance things out. Taking liver support like Release oil, Juva Cleanse or Juva Tone can also help take care of excess estrogen.

If you are having a lot of estrogen deficiency problems like low libido or dryness of the vagina, support the adrenal more during the first half of the cycle. And use more Progessence Plus the second half of the cycle. Also use more Thyromin and Ultra Young Spray to see if this assists these problems. Claraderm is a fantastic product to use for dry vagina problems.

On days 19-23 use more Progessence Plus around this peak. If you feel like you need more, the next month work day 18-24 or 17-25 etc.

Water retention is caused by lack of progesterone and pituitary inadequacy. Weight gain originates in the thyroid and adrenals, so support those organs. Heat problems are come from the thyroid and from excess estrogen. Chills may also be trace to the thyroid.

## Bleeding off and on continually

Clean the uterus by drinking 2 teaspoons of blue vervain tincture in a class of water every day for three days. Repeat a week later. Start using Progessence Plus and balance it with Femigen and Estro as needed.

## Heavy Bleeding

This may arise from a variety of issues. It may stem from low progesterone and/or low estrogen. Other potential causes include fibroids, polyps and cysts. Progesterone Plus will assist in clearing these problems. You also may not be getting enough calcium, with the result that your blood is not clotting well. It would be worthwhile to increase your calcium intake by taking calcium citrate or getting it from plant foods to see if that helps resolve the problem. You may want to consult your physician if these ideas don't take care of the issue or in any case if it is severe.

**Facial hair**

This is caused by either two much testosterone or too little progesterone, or else the adrenal is not successfully converting androsterone to the female hormones. Use Progessence Plus and support the adrenal daily with Omega Oils, Trace Minerals, Super B, Nutmeg, Clove or Endo Flex. It would be wise to do a colon cleanse and a liver cleanse so the liver will be able to rid the body of excess hormones.

**Low sex drive**

Add 1- 3 drops of Mister oil around day 15 by mouth or around your ankles. Sometimes just smelling it will do the trick. Mister boosts the male hormone testosterone, but women also need just a little bit of testosterone every month. Support the pituitary gland and the thyroid and use more Progessence Plus. Claraderm assists with low sex drive when sprayed directly into the vagina. Lower your stress by using such oils as Tranquil, Valor or Peace and Calming and supporting the adrenal glands.

**Excess sex drive**

Cleanse your liver to make sure you don't have excess hormones floating in the system that the liver isn't removing. Increase estrogen during your period and especially during day 10. Increased estrogen has been said to lower sex drive in some females while others claim that it increases their sex drive.

Unfortunately, each woman differs in what is causing her excess sex drive so you will have to experiment with the hormones to see which works for you. Between day 11 and day 17 a woman should naturally have an increased sex drive as it is her body's way of signaling that it is ready to get pregnant.

**Uterus cleansing**

At times a woman might have discharges or a heavy feeling in her uterus area. I recommend cleaning out the uterus if you are having these difficulties and also after every miscarriage or pregnancy. The Master Cleanse is a great way to clean the uterus. I have also had my patients use blue vervain tincture over the years, mixing 1/3 oz. of tincture with one cup warm water and drinking it all at once, once a day for three days.

**Baby blues**

Start Ultra Young + spray and 1 tsp of essential fatty acids like Omega Blues 3x a day about a month before the baby is due. During the last month of development a fetus requires a lot of essential fatty acids to develop its brain. If they are not available in the mother's diet the baby will take fatty acids from where they are most readily available, which is the mother's brain. By increasing essential fatty acids such as flax seed oil or the omega-3 fish oils, mothers have experienced a decrease in post-partum depression.

One week before the baby is due, use a lot of Clary Sage or its blends around the ankles and take several drops a day by mouth. While in labor increase the Clary Sage or its blends to several drops an hour. As soon as the baby is born put some Progessence Plus on your neck. It is safe to use during breast feeding and will not harm the baby even if it is a boy. Continue use as needed for mood swings.

Continue using the Ultra Young + spray and taking fatty acids. You can also add B vitamins, trace minerals and calcium along with Joy oil and Peace and Calming oil. The B vitamins, minerals and calcium support the adrenal glands and the nervous systems while the essential oils give the emotions a well-deserved lift.

**Low milk supply for lactating mothers**

Support the Pituitary Gland with Ultra Young + Spray. Also feed the body Essential Fatty Acids, drink lots of water and plenty of protein. Rest!!!! It is great to feed the body what I call the cow diet for several days. That is feed yourself anything that you would feed a cow to produce milk! Oats, oats and more oats! It can be in any form including granola and cookies!

Please note that the information presented in this publication is not intended to treat any disease and does not replace a doctor's diagnosis. It is given for educational purposes only. Although Young Living oils are mentioned and recommended in this publication, it has not been approved by Young Living Oils, Inc. and is strictly the responsibility of the author.

If you would like more information to know more about your personal hormone cycle or other health matters please contact me at http://doctorleanne.com/talk-to-dr-leanne/ phone-consultation/ and order a Hormone Assessment. I will then send you out a symptom survey to see how I can assist you to better health.

Natural supplements and bio-identical hormones, diet and exercise, as well as detoxification methods, give you the best chance of balancing your body and regaining your youthful energy. Create a healthy lifestyle that keeps you active for many years! With the right information, you can make choices to support and improve your health the way nature intended. You don't have to feel worn out and tired anymore. Tame the dragon within you. Get your natural energy back and start feeling good again - today!

**If you need help knowing how to balance your hormones. Go to** http://doctorleanne.com/talk-to-dr-leanne/phone-consultation/ **and purchase either a Personal Consultation or a Hormone Assessment package.**

# The Dragon Menu:

What to feed your dragon to keep it alive, healthy and docile: (purr)

**For Pituitary Support:**
- FISH!!! oils Like Omega Blues
- Ultra Young Spray +
- Sacred Frankincense

**For Thyroid Support:**
- Thyromin and Ultra Young Spray
- Myrtle Oil

**For Adrenal Support:**
- Fish oil like Omega Blues 1 tbs/day (Yummy, I love fish!)
- Super B and Mineral Essence
- Prenolone Cream or PD 80/20 to assist with hormonal building blocks

**For everyday support of the entire body:**
- Progessence plus
- Femigen

## That's better

Before using Progessence Plus, I was constantly tired, I ached all over, I had fibromyalgia, I had had several heart attacks and strokes, I had inflamed veins and arteries. I had constant migraines. I had terrible PMS (cramps, headaches, nausea, heavy bleeding). I didn't have hot flashes as much as I felt I lived in a constant furnace. I had miserable night sweats. I had ascites. I had edema in the ankles. I slept poorly. The doctors diagnosed me with Lupus. Not due to the Lupus blood factor but due to history of symptoms. It seemed I had them all. I was miserable and figured I was dying a slow death.

I started Progessence Plus about two weeks after the Young Living Convention in June 2010. At first, it was as if I was on a bucking bronco. My hormones and mood swings as well as hot flashes and migraines increased. If I thought I was in a furnace before, someone turned up the heat! But I stuck it out. I started increasing my Progessence plus. I followed the days of the Female Chart and took other supplements as outlined. I wasn't going to give up! About four months later, I began to notice more energy. Now 6 months have gone by. Most of the above symptoms are gone. My lupus mask is gone. My body is cooling down. I have tons of energy and have been able to get all kinds of things done! I can focus and think more clearly. My heavy bleeding has disappeared. I have fewer headaches. My fibromyalgia is gone. Now suddenly, my body is beginning to let go of excess weight. Without doing anything different, with in the last few weeks I have released 15 pounds.

I am going to continue on this program until I know that my body has completely healed from lack of progesterone for too many years! Don't give up! What I found that balances me is one Thyromin daily and one or two sprays two times a day of Ultra Young Spray+ except during days 8-14 of my period then I take two Thyromin and increase the Ultra Young Spray+ to several times a day. Two drops of Progessence Plus rubbed every two hours on my wrists daily. There are days I feel to take more.

Keep it up! The body is healing what it needs to heal first to survive then it will begin to heal what you feel is the most important next!

Taming your inner dragon every day by taking care of your hormones, along with the right food, the right exercise and the right amount of rest will allow you to lead a nice, gentle, more human life. You'll be happier, and so will those around you!